Discovering Literature Series

A Teaching Guide to

The Outsiders

by Jeanette Machoian

Illustration by Kathy Kifer and Marina Krasnik

The Outsiders
Puffin Books
Published by the Penguin Group
Penguin Puffin Inc., 375 Hudson St.
New York, New York 10014

Published by:
Garlic Press
605 Powers St.
Eugene, OR 97402

ISBN 978-0-931993-93-0
Order Number GP-093
Printed in China

www.garlicpress.com

Table of Contents

The Discovering Literature Series is designed to develop a student's appreciation for good literature and to improve reading comprehension. While many skills reinforce a student's ability to comprehend what he or she reads (sequencing, cause and effect, finding details, using context clues), two skills are vital. They are: discerning **main ideas** and **summarizing** text. Students who can master these two essential skills develop into sophisticated readers.

The following discussion details the various elements that constitute this Series.

About Chapter Organization

Sample: Chapter 1, with Student Directives, Chapter Vocabulary, and Chapter Summary

Each chapter analysis is organized into three basic elements: **Student Directives**, **Chapter Vocabulary**, and **Chapter Summary**. Student Directives and Chapter Vocabulary need to be displayed on the board or on an overhead projector after each chapter is read. Students copy the Chapter Vocabulary and write their own summaries following the Student Directives.

The **Student Directives** contain the main ideas in each chapter. They provide the students, working individually or in groups, with a framework for developing their summaries. Student Directives can also be used as group discussion topics.

The **Chapter Vocabulary** includes definitions of key words from each chapter. To save time, students need only to copy, not look up, definitions. Suggestions for teaching vocabulary to students are as follows:

1. Make and display flashcards with the words and definitions. Refer to vocabulary cards in daily review.
2. Have students write sentences individually, in groups, or as a class using the words in the story's context.
3. Give frequent quizzes before an actual test.
4. Have students make their own vocabulary crossword puzzles or word search puzzles.
5. Play 20 questions with vocabulary words.
6. Host a vocabulary bee where the students give definitions for the word rather than spelling it.

A **Chapter Summary** for each chapter is included for teacher use and knowledge. Some students may initially need to copy the summaries in order to feel comfortable writing their own subsequent ones. Other students can use the completed sum-

Sample:
Blackline Master

maries as a comparison to guide their own work. Summary writing provides an opportunity to polish student composition skills, in addition to reading skills.

The **blackline master**, *Chapter Summary & Vocabulary*, is provided on page 47. It can be duplicated for student use. Teachers can also use it to make transparencies for displaying Student Directives and Chapter Vocabulary.

In addition, teachers may opt to have students make folders to house their Chapter Summary & Vocabulary sheets. A sample cover sheet (see page 49) for student embellishments has been provided. Cover sheets can be laminated, if desired, and affixed to a manila (or other) folder.

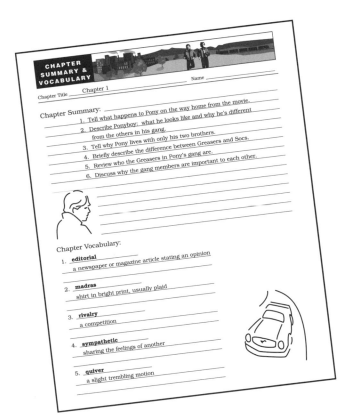

Sample Transparency:
Student Directives and Chapter Vocabulary

Sample Transparency:
Chapter Summary and Chapter Vocabulary

The above two samples serve to illustrate how the **blackline master**, *Chapter Summary & Vocabulary*, can be used as a transparency to focus student work. These transparencies are particularly effective for displaying Student Directives and Chapter Vocabulary. They are also effective for initially modeling how Chapter Summaries can be written.

About the Skill Pages

Sample: Skill Pag

Skill Pages throughout the series have been developed to increase students' understanding of various literary elements and to reinforce vital reading skills. Since the entire series is devoted to reinforcing **main ideas** and **summarizing** skills, no further work has been provided on these skills. Depending upon each novel, Skill Pages reinforce various skills from among the following: **outlining**; **cause and effect**; **sequencing**; **character**, **setting**, **and plot development**; and **figurative language**. You will note that character development is based upon a values framework.

About the Tests

Sample: Test

At the end of each five-chapter block, a comprehensive open-book **Test** has been developed for your use. Each test includes reading comprehension, vocabulary, and short essays.

An Answer Key is provided at the back of the book for each Test.

The vocabulary portion of the Tests may be particularly difficult. You will probably want to give one or two vocabulary quizzes before administering each of the six Tests.

About the Writer's Forum

Sample: Writer's Forum

Suggestions for writing are presented under the **Writer's Forum** throughout this guide. You can choose from these suggestions or substitute your own creative-writing ideas.

Student Directives

1. Relate what happens to Pony on the way home from the movie.
2. Tell why Pony lives with only his two brothers, and his relationship with them.
3. Briefly describe the Greasers in Pony's gang.
4. Discuss why the gang members are important to each other.
5. Describe Pony at school.

Vocabulary

editorial	a newspaper or magazine article stating an opinion
madras	light cotton shirt in a bright print, usually plaid
rivalry	competition
sympathetic	sharing the feelings of another
quiver	a slight trembling motion
reputation	the character of someone as seen by others
suspicious	showing distrust

Summary

The Outsiders begins when Ponyboy Curtis is jumped as he walks home from the movie theater. The Socs, or rich kids, circle Pony, hit him, and hold a knife to his head, threatening to cut his hair. When he yells, his gang, the Greasers, shows up. The reader learns about Pony and his gang as Pony tells the story. Pony's parents were killed in a car accident so he lives with his two brothers. Darry, his oldest brother, is a hard worker. He is serious and stern with Pony and tries to keep Pony on the right track. Pony doesn't think Darry cares for him. Soda, the middle brother, is just the opposite. He's fun-loving and seems to understand Pony's feelings. Pony feels close to Soda and looks up to him. Soda has dropped out of high school and calls himself "dumb." Other gang members are Steve, Soda's best friend; Two-Bit, the clown of the gang; Dallas, the toughest member who also has a police record; and Johnny, the gang's pet, small and quiet. The Greasers think of each other as family and stick together. They like to appear tough to others. Pony wonders if the Socs have the same feelings and if their girlfriends are similar to the girls the Greasers know. He thinks about this as he does his homework. Pony is a good student and is put in "A" classes, although he feels judged by and different from the other students.

About the Characters

Directions: Below is a Character Chart to help you organize the characters from the novel. Fill in whatever information is missing—either the character's name or a character summary.

Ponyboy	Darry	Two-Bit	Dally
Sodapop	Johnny	Steve	

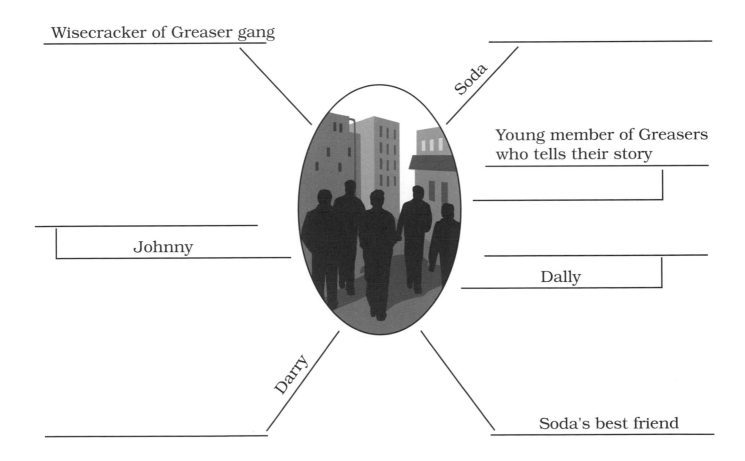

Wisecracker of Greaser gang

Soda

Young member of Greasers who tells their story

Johnny

Dally

Darry

Soda's best friend

Student Directives

1. Describe Dally's behavior at the drive-in movie theater.
2. Tell why Pony and Johnny end up sitting next to Marcia and Cherry.
3. Review why Johnny is so nervous all the time.
4. Discuss why Cherry says that things are rough all over.

Vocabulary

hastily	done or made in a hurry
incredulous	feeling disbelief
hesitation	a pause because of forgetfulness or uncertainty
hoodlum	a rowdy destructive adolescent
stricken	overcome by emotion
muffle	to lessen the sound of
rebellious	opposing authority
rumble	a fight between gangs

Summary

Pony and Johnny sneak into a drive-in with Dally. They sit behind two Soc girls, Cherry and Marcia. Dally talks rudely to them until the girls become very angry and Dally leaves. Pony and Johnny, at the request of the girls, move up to sit with them since the girls are alone. They had left their boyfriends because the boys were drinking. Two-Bit shows up to watch the movie, too. When they go for popcorn, Pony explains to Cherry why Johnny is so nervous: Johnny was beat severely by the Socs. Cherry tries to convince Pony that all Socs are not alike and that even the Socs have troubles. This makes Pony think because he knows that not all the Greasers would do things that Dally would.

Stereotyping

Have you ever looked at someone who was dressed a certain way, or who lived in a particular area of town, or who had a certain group of friends or who always earned good or poor grades...and assumed something about that person's life or personality? Maybe this has happened to you.

This is called stereotyping. An early example from the Outsiders occurs in the assumptions that the Socs and Greasers have about each other. Each group believes or assumes that members of the rival group are indistinguishable from one another. When they stereotype the members of the other group, they disregard the uniqueness of each member.

Pony and Cherry have a conversation in which we see assumptions that can be made about each other. Pony talks about the Socs as though they are like those boys who beat up Johnny. Cherry tries to convince him that this isn't true, using Dally as an example. She knows that Dally might mug someone, but Pony would not. Pony and Dally belong to the same gang, but that does not mean they are just alike in character.

At this point, Pony also believes that the Greasers are the only ones with any problems. He thinks that because the Socs all have money and opportunities, they must not have any problems. Cherry tells him that "things are rough all over." Cherry seems to realize this truth, but most of the Socs and Greasers do not. This leads to conflicts between the two groups.

Explain why you think stereotyping leads to conflicts between people and groups of people. Use an experience you or someone close to you has had as an example of your explanation.

Student Directives

1. Tell where Pony, Johnny, Two-Bit, Marcia, and Cherry are going when the Socs drive by.

2. Discuss what Cherry sees as the main difference between the Socs and the Greasers, and why she and Pony are the same.

3. Tell where Pony and Johnny go after Cherry and Marcia leave with their boyfriends.

4. Describe what happens when Pony finally gets home.

Vocabulary

gallant	brave, noble
rank	having a bad smell/taste; position in a classification
sophisticated	not natural or simple; worldly
aloof	acting distant; indifferent
elite	a socially superior group
tension	strain, unrest
resignedly	giving in without complaint
reeling	staggering or swaying

Summary

Pony, Johnny, Two-Bit, Cherry, and Marcia start walking to Two-Bit's house. They plan to pick up Two-Bit's car and drive Cherry and Marcia home. Along the way, Pony and Cherry talk. Pony decides that money is what separates Greasers and Socs. Cherry says it's more than money; it's also emotion—greasers have it and Socs don't. Pony and Cherry realize that they are largely the same as they watch the same sunset. A blue Mustang pulls up and the girls' boyfriends, Bob and Randy, get out. A fight is avoided when Cherry and Marcia agree to ride home with their boyfriends. Later, in the vacant lot, Pony is awakened by Johnny. They had intended to watch the stars before Pony's midnight curfew, but fell asleep while talking about a place without groups like Greasers and Socs. Pony gets home long after midnight and an argument erupts between Darry and Pony. He runs back to the lot, telling Johnny they will run away together. Running several blocks and talking with Johnny brings Pony's senses back. He decides to walk to the park and then return home.

The Socs and the Greasers are different in several ways, especially from outward appearances. However, Pony discovers that they are also alike in many ways. List as many differences and similarities as you can from the novel. Some examples are given to get you started.

SOCS		GREASERS
Differences	*Similarities*	*Differences*
Soc girls don't act tough		Greaser girls act tough
	Both can get good grades	

Family

One theme in *The Outsiders* is the importance of people in your life who care about you. This is one reason young people join gangs. Pony tells Johnny, "You got the whole gang." Johnny replies, "It ain't the same as having your own folks care about you." Later, Pony understands and agrees with this. He decides that even Soda and Darry can't take the place of parents.

If Johnny explained this further in a journal entry, what would he say? Why aren't friends and brothers the same as having parents who care about you? Write a journal entry for Johnny, giving details and further explanations. Then, add an example from your own life to help show the importance of parents.

Student Directives

1. Describe what happens when the Socs show up at the park.
2. Tell where Pony and Johnny go when they leave the park.
3. Relate Dally's reaction to their news.
4. Discuss how Pony and Johnny are feeling by the time they get to the old church, and how they feel when they get there.

Vocabulary

defiance	open refusal to obey
contempt	scorn; lack of respect
panic	sudden overpowering fear
apprehensive	fearful or worried
self-preservation	taking care of or saving oneself
rueful	filled with regret or pity
premonition	a feeling that something is going to happen

Summary

Pony and Johnny are sitting in the park when five Socs show up. Filled with fear, they have no time to get away. The Socs had been drinking and after exchanging insults with Pony, the Socs shove his head in the park's fountain. Pony passes out. When he awakens, Pony finds that Johnny has killed the Soc who tried to drown him. Johnny is calmer than Pony and suggests they seek Dally for help. They find Dally at a party where he gives them money, a gun, and directions to an abandoned church in the country. They sneak onto a train and arrive at Jay Mountain early in the morning. Although tired, numb and hungry, they make it into the church and fall fast asleep.

Elements of a Narrative

Stories, whether short stories or long novels, have certain main elements which make them easily read and understood, as well as interesting.

One main element is the **character**: the person or people the story is about. The author of a novel shows a character's personality by the things the character does, says, and thinks, as well as through description.

Another element is **setting**: the where and when of a story; the place and time a story takes place. The author may make this element very clear at the beginning of a story, or the reader will have to discover it through inference.

Yet another element is **conflict**–often more than one conflict. Conflict revolves around a problem or problems a character has with another character, with society, with nature, or even with himself or herself. The story largely centers around conflicts, which are often resolved by the end of the novel.

Possibly the most complex narrative element is the **plot**. To develop the plot, the author must carefully plan a sequence of events that will hold the reader's interest. The author must concentrate on only the important aspects of the story so that it doesn't drag on. Additionally, the events must present a problem that the central character must resolve.

S.E. Hinton, the author of *The Outsiders*, presents all of these elements in such a way that makes the story flow interestingly, as well as clearly.

Elements of a Narrative Outline

Directions: Study the basic elements from your reading so far. Complete the following outline.

Main Character   Describe Ponyboy.

A. _____
   _____
B. _____
   _____
C. _____
   _____

Setting   Describe the place and time of the story.

A. Where:_____
   _____
B. When: _____
   _____

Conflicts   Describe the main problems with which the character deals.

A. _____
   _____
B. _____
   _____
C. _____
   _____

Plot   From your reading so far, tell how you think the events will develop.

A. _____
   _____
B. _____
   _____
C. _____

Cause and Effect

Directions: Match the correct effect with its cause by placing the correct letter in the blank.

A **Cause** produces a result	An **Effect** results from a cause
1. Pony did not think of asking someone to go to the movies with him._____	A. he got his nickname, Two-Bit.
2. Because he thinks he is "dumb", _____	B. they dream of a place where there are no social classes, just people.
3. Because he always had something to say,_____	C. Pony decides to run away.
4. Johnny had been beaten badly by Socs, so_____	D. Darry gets upset at Pony when he gets jumped.
5. When Johnny told him to leave Marcia and Cherry alone,_____	E. he reminds her that he watches sunsets, too.
6. When Cherry says she can't talk to Pony at school,_____	F. Dally left the theater angrily.
7. Because Pony and Johnny are tired of Socs having all the breaks,_____	G. they went looking for a fight.
8. Pony fell asleep in the lot, and _____	H. then he got into an argument with Darry once he got home.
9. The Socs were drunk and angry because their girlfriends left them at the drive-in, so_____	I. Soda drops out of school.
10. Johnny was afraid for Pony's life, so_____	J. he was even more nervous all the time.
11. After Darry hits Pony in anger,_____	K. he stabbed the Soc.

Name _____

Multiple Choice

Directions:

Circle the letter of the correct answer.

1. Pony has gone to the movies alone because...

   A. no one else could go.

   B. Pony believes no one else likes movies the way he does.

   C. Pony thought he would meet someone there.

2. According to Soda, he dropped out of school because...

   A. he's dumb.

   B. he needed to work for Pony's sake.

   C. he wanted to prove he could hold a job.

3. Pony was embarrassed when Dally started talking to the girls at the drive-in because...

   A. they were not greasy girls.

   B. they were older girls.

   C. they were related to Two-Bit.

4. Dally let Johnny tell him to stop pestering Cherry and Marcia because...

   A. Dally always took Johnny's advice.

   B. Johnny is the gang's pet.

   C. Johnny is tougher than Dally.

5. When Two-Bit comes up behind Pony and Johnny at the drive-in, Johnny feels

   A. silly.

   B. frightened

   C. happy.

6. Cherry and Pony...

   A. tell each other things they couldn't tell others.

   B. become best buddies.

   C. leave the drive-in angry at each other.

7. Johnny and Pony dream of a place...

   A. where they wouldn't have to go to school.

   B. where they could make lots of money.

   C. without Greasers and Socs.

8. When Pony gets home late, Darry...

   A. tells Pony to go to bed.

   B. hits Pony when they argue.

   C. gets mad at Pony for not doing his chores.

9. After Bob is murdered, Dally...

   A. takes Johnny and Pony to a place to sleep.

   B. tells Johnny and Pony how to disguise themselves.

   C. gives Johnny and Pony money and tells them where to hide.

10. When Pony gets to the country, he knows he won't like it as much as he thought because...

   A. he has to hide and can't see anyone.

   B. there are more people than he thought living there.

   C. it turns out that some Socs live there.

Vocabulary

Directions:

Fill in the blank with the correct word.

rivalry	hastily	resignedly
reputation	gallant	defiance
suspicious	rank	apprehensive
hesitation		

1. _____ a pause because of forgetfulness or uncertainty

2. _____ brave, noble

3. _____ fearful or worried

Name _____

4. _____   giving in without complaint

5. _____   a competition

6. _____   done or made in a hurry

7. _____   character of a person as seen by others

8. _____   showing distrust

9. _____   open refusal to obey

10. _____   having a bad smell or taste

Essay Questions

Directions:

Answer in complete

sentences.

1. The Greasers are known to be mean and tough. Name several things about Pony that make him different from his reputation.

   _____

   _____

   _____

2. Explain why it seems to Pony that Darry doesn't care for him.

   _____

   _____

   _____

3. Name two reasons why the Socs went looking for Pony and Johnny.

   _____

   _____

   _____

Student Directives

1. Explain why Pony imagines all kinds of bad possibilities while he waits for Johnny to return with supplies.
2. Tell what Pony and Johnny do to disguise themselves.
3. Explain why the disguise is depressing to them.
4. Describe what Pony and Johnny do to pass time.
5. Review the news that Dally brings to Pony and Johnny.

Vocabulary

implore	to ask humbly; to beg
tuft	a small bunch or clump of something
sullen	not sociable; gloomy
clenched	held tightly
hue	a shade of a color
subside	to become lower or less
elude	to avoid or escape
indignant	angry because of something unjust

Summary

Ponyboy wakes up late in the afternoon. He tries to pretend that he's at home and it's a normal weekend. While he waits for Johnny to return to the church with supplies, he lets his imagination run away with him and he worries about their situation. Johnny returns with food and other supplies, including the materials necessary to cut their hair, wash it, and bleach Pony's. When they finish, they become further depressed–long greasy hair is so important to the Greaser. Johnny and Pony talk and cry, easing their nerves. They spend the next few days reading *Gone With the Wind* and playing poker. They watched the sunrise one morning and discussed Robert Frost's poem "Nothing Gold Can Stay." Pony and Johnny decide that they are different from others because they can understand such things. Dally appears on the fifth day with news from home and a letter from Soda. He takes them out for something to eat and tells them that a rumble is planned for the next night: Socs against Greasers. Two-Bit had been jumped, but is okay. Other news includes the fact that Cherry has become a spy for the Greasers.

Figurative Language - Metaphors

Authors often use figurative language to make their writing interesting and more meaningful to the reader. One type of figurative language is the metaphor. A metaphor, stating that one thing is the other, makes a comparison between two unlike things. For example, Pony describes Dally's eyes in this way: "His eyes were blue, blazing ice....." Dally's eyes are being compared to ice because he looks at people coldly and with hate.

In Chapter 5, Pony quotes Robert Frost's poem "Nothing Gold Can Stay." Frost makes use of the metaphor to communicate his message about young people. He begins by writing that nature's first green, things such as new plants, trees, grass and especially young people, are gold.

Directions: Answer the following questions to assist you in understanding metaphors and, in particular, Frost's meaning about youth.

Metaphor examples:

1. The statement "Her words were sugar" is a metaphor. Her words are being compared to sugar. What is being said about her words?

2. "It's raining cats and dogs" is a metaphor. The rain is being compared to cats and dogs. What is being said about the rain?

3. "He is my fortress": To what is "He" being compared? What is being said about him?

"Nothing Gold Can Stay":

4. Gold is a precious, and expensive, metal. What comparison can be made between "nature's first green" and gold?

5. Another metaphor in Frost's poem is "Her early leaf's a flower." Explain how nature's "early leaf," or someone's youth, can be like a flower.

6. How is the youth of someone's life "gold"?

Student Directives

1. Tell why Cherry becomes a spy for the Greasers.
2. Relate the decision that Johnny makes.
3. Discuss Dally's advice to Johnny about his parents.
4. Describe what the boys find when they return to the church.
5. Review the heroic actions of Pony, Johnny, and Dally.

Vocabulary

testify	to make a statement under oath
grim	harsh in appearance; stern
apparent	open to view; appearing to be true
aim	to intend; to direct toward a goal
conviction	strong belief; the act of being found guilty of a crime
scowl	frown or angry look
towheaded	having soft, blond hair
fiend	very wicked or cruel person

Summary

Chapter Six begins with Dally explaining how Cherry feels like the whole mess is her fault and that she wants to keep the Greasers informed about the rumble from the Socs' side. She even says she'll testify that Bob, Randy, and the others were drinking and that Johnny acted in self-defense. When Johnny announces to Dally that he wants to turn himself in, Dally is angry but finally agrees. In a rare moment for Dally, he tells Johnny he doesn't want jail to harden Johnny as it did him. Johnny wants to know if his parents have asked about him. Dally says "no" and insists Johnny shouldn't care about his parents, because the gang cares about him. When they get back to the church, it is on fire. As Dally protests, Pony and Johnny get out of the car and run toward the fire. Once there, they discover that picnicking school children are inside the church. Pony and Johnny enter to get them, not thinking of their own safety. As they get the last child out, the church begins to collapse. Pony gets out, but timber falls on Johnny's back. Dally goes in after Johnny. Pony passes out. Once at the hospital, Pony, bruised and tired, awaits word on Dally and Johnny.

Student Directives

1. Relate Dally's and Johnny's conditions.
2. Describe the mood in the Curtis home on Pony's first morning back.
3. Review what the newspaper says about the Greasers and especially the Curtis' brothers.
4. Briefly discuss Pony's conversation with Randy.
5. Tell how Pony views Randy after they talk.

Vocabulary

radiate	shine; to spread from a center
bleak	not hopeful or encouraging
plead	to offer as a defense; to beg
mourn	to feel or show grief
drawl	to speak slowly, holding vowel sounds longer than usual
cocksure	complete assurance; overconfident
aghast	struck with terror or amazement
exploit	a brave or daring act

Summary

Darry and Soda join Pony in the waiting room at the hospital where they are swarmed by police and reporters asking questions. When the police and reporters finally leave, the brothers learn of Dally's and Johnny's conditions. Dally will be fine in a few days, but Johnny, with a broken back and bad burns, will be crippled if he lives. The mood at home the next morning was sleepy until Steve and Two-Bit barged in with the newspaper. The newspaper called Johnny and Pony heroes, but Pony also learned that he must appear in juvenile court for running away and that Johnny is charged with manslaughter. Two-Bit and Pony walk to the Tasty Freeze where Randy (a Soc) asks to talk to Pony. He talks about Bob being a good buddy and how Bob wished that someone would set limits for him. Randy tells Pony that he isn't going to the rumble because he is tired of the whole situation and he knows the rumble won't change it. From their conversation, Pony realizes that Socs are just people, too, and that they do, indeed, have their own problems.

Student Directives

1. Tell about Pony and Two-Bit's visit with Johnny in the hospital.
2. Describe Johnny's feelings about dying.
3. Discuss Johnny's reaction to his mother's visit.
4. Relate why Dally is so angry when Two-Bit and Pony leave the hospital.
5. What was Two-Bit's reaction to Pony's concerns about the rumble.
6. Discuss Pony and Cherry's conversation about Bob and Johnny.

Vocabulary

expression   a way of speaking that shows one's mood

abrupt   happening without warning; sudden

resemblance   likeness or similarity

divert   to turn attention away; distract

reluctant   showing doubt or unwillingness

dogged   stubbornly determined

desperate   being beyond hope; causing despair

Summary

Pony and Two-Bit go to the hospital to see Johnny, who realizes how bad his condition is. He wants a new copy of *Gone With the Wind*. Pony tries to be cheerful and silently commands himself not to cry. He tells Johnny the same, realizing that life on the streets has taught them how to shut off their emotions. Johnny now knows he doesn't want to die yet. When Johnny's mother comes to the hospital, he refuses to see her and passes out. She stands in the hallway complaining and blames Pony and Two-Bit when they come out of the room. When they get to Dally's room, his ornery behavior tells them he's okay. He's angry about missing the rumble and worried about Johnny, although he doesn't voice his concern in those words. As they wait for a bus home, Pony admits he feels sick but makes Two-Bit promise not to tell Darry. Pony tries to tell Two-Bit why he's worried about the rumble, but Two-Bit pretends to not understand. Cherry meets them at the lot and assures them that the Socs plan on using no weapons. Pony speaks harshly to Cherry when she says she won't go see Johnny and starts to walk away, but he turns back and asks her if she can see the sunset well from the West as he can from the East. They part friends.

Sequencing

Event 1: _Pony is jumped._

Event 2: _____

Event 3: _____

Event 4: _____

Event 5: _Darry hits Pony._

Event 6: _____

Event 7: _____

Event 8: _____

Event 9: _____

Event 10: _____

Event 11: _Darry, Soda, and Pony are interviewed for the newspaper._

Event 12: _____

Event 13: _____

Event 14: _____

Event 15: _____

Directions:
Organize the events from Chapters 1-8 in the order they occurred. Three events have been listed for you.

- Dally gives Pony and Johnny money and directions.
- Pony and Johnny fall asleep in the lot.
- Pony is jumped.
- Two-Bit and Pony visit Johnny in the hospital.
- Pony and Johnny go to Windrixville.
- Pony and Johnny run to the park.
- Two-Bit, Johnny, and Pony start to take Cherry and Marcia home.
- Dally, Johnny, and Pony go to the movies.
- Dally asks for Two-Bit's switchblade.
- The Socs hold Pony's head underwater.
- Pony and Johnny save some kids.
- Two-Bit and Pony meet Cherry in the vacant lot.
- Randy talks to Pony.
- Darry hits Pony.
- Darry, Soda, and Pony are interviewed for the newspaper.

Identifying Characters

Directions: Use the following list to choose the character by whom the quote was said. Names can be used more than once.

Pony	Dally
Darry	Johnny
Soda	Two-Bit
Steve	Cherry

_____ 1. "No, Johnny, not my hair!" (p. 71)

_____ 2. "I wish you'd come back and turn yourselfves [sic] in..." (p. 82)

_____ 3. "I couldn't tell Dally that I hated to shoot things." (p. 86)

_____ 4. "I guess we ruined our hair for nothing..." (p. 89)

_____ 5. "Oh, Pony, I thought we'd lost you..." (p. 98)

_____ 6. "Work? And ruin my rep?" (p. 112)

_____ 7. "I'm scared stiff. I used to talk about killing myself..." (p. 121)

_____ 8. "We gotta get even with the Socs. For Johnny." (p. 125)

_____ 9. "They play your way. No weapons, fair deal. Your rules." (p. 128)

_____ 10. "I'm really home in bed,..." (p. 68)

_____ 11. "Would you rather have me living in hide-outs for the rest of my life, always on the run?" (p. 90)

_____ 12. "They'd never believe a greasey-lookin' mug could be a hero." (p. 107)

_____ 13. "...if the fuzz show, you two beat it out of there. The rest of us can only get jailed." (p. 137)

_____ 14. "This house ain't messy. You oughtta see my house." (p. 114)

_____ 15. "Don't you know a rumble ain't a rumble unless I'm in it?" (p. 144)

_____ 16. "You smoke more than a pack today and I'll skin you." (p. 113)

_____ 17. "Oh, Ponyboy, your hair...your tuff, tuff hair..." (p. 97)

_____ 18. "You don't know what a few months in jail can do to you." (p. 89)

_____ 19. "I've got to cut out smoking or I won't make track next year." (p. 112)

_____ 20. "I know I'm too young to be in love and all that, but Bob was something special." (p. 129)

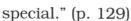

Writing About Yourself

When they first meet and talk, Cherry tells Ponyboy that the Socs have problems that the Greasers have never even heard about. Pony better understands this after he talks to Randy (p. 115–118).

What are some of the problems that the Greasers have?

What are some of the problems that the Socs have?

Have you ever believed that one of your classmates or someone you know had no problems because they had money or were popular or smart? Sometimes, like Pony and his friends, you may think only you have any troubles. Choose an incident that happened to you or someone close to you that made you aware of the fact that no one's life is without some difficulties, no matter how easy some people's lives may seem. Or maybe you read a book that helped you realize this important truth. Write about what you learned and how you may see yourself or your life more positively now.

TEST

Name _____

Multiple Choice

Directions:

Circle the letter of the correct answer.

1. Pony and Johnny pass time at the church by
   A. playing checkers.
   B. reading *Gone With the Wind.*
   C. reading a book of poems.

2. Pony doesn't want Johnny to cut his hair because
   A. Soda told Pony not to cut his hair.
   B. long hair was the Greasers' trademark.
   C. it would make him look too old.

3. At the church, when Pony and Johnny talk about the night of the murder,
   A. they cry until they get used to the situation.
   B. they decide together to go home.
   C. they argue and blame each other.

4. Johnny sees Dally as gallant because
   A. he admires Dally's manners.
   B. Dally took the blame for something Two-Bit did.
   C. Dally tells the truth.

5. Johnny tells Dally that
   A. he admires him.
   B. Cherry Valance wants to help the Greasers.
   C. he's going to turn himself in.

6. While Pony waits at the hospital, Soda and Darry come in.
   A. They are angry at Pony for running away.
   B. Pony finally realizes that Darry does care about him.
   C. They all go home right away.

7. When the newspaper comes out the next morning, Pony
   A. tries to hide the picture because of his hair.
   B. finds out he's being blamed for the murder.
   C. finds out there will be a hearing and he might have to go to a boys' home.

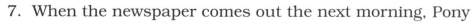

Name _____

8. Randy won't be in the rumble because he

    A. misses Bob too much.

    B. is scared.

    C. is sick of fighting.

9. After Pony talks to Randy, he

    A. begins to see Randy as a real person, not just a Soc.

    B. hates Randy more than ever.

    C. blames Randy for everything.

10. Johnny says that he's not ready to die because

    A. he thinks being a hero is fun.

    B. he wants to become a fireman.

    C. there's a lot he has not seen or done.

Vocabulary

Directions:

Fill in the blank with the correct word.

sullen	grim	scowl
hue	conviction	aghast
elude	fiend	divert
indignant		

1. _____ not sociable; gloomy

2. _____ strong belief; the act of being found guilty of a crime

3. _____ to turn attention away; distract

4. _____ struck with terror or amazement

5. _____ harsh in appearance; stern

6. _____ angry because of something unjust

7. _____ a very wicked or cruel person

8. _____ frown or angry look

9. _____ a shade of a color

10. _____ to avoid or escape

Chapters 5-8, Page 3   Name _____

Essay Questions

Directions:

Answer in complete

sentences.

1. Tell why Jerry Wood has a hard time believing that Pony, Johnny, and Dally are Greasers in trouble with the law. Use information from the book to complete your answer.

_____

_____

_____

2. Why does Cherry become a spy for the Greasers? Give information from the novel to support your answer.

_____

_____

_____

Student Directives

1. Why do Darry, Soda, and Pony clean up before a rumble.

2. Explain why Darry is concerned about Pony participating in this rumble.

3. Discuss the reasons that the different gang members fight.

4. Describe the observation Pony makes just before the rumble starts.

5. Review Dally's ideas of how to avoid getting hurt.

6. Discuss Johnny's reaction to the outcome of the rumble and his advice to Pony.

Vocabulary

wearily	showing loss of strength
prime	first in importance, rank, or quality
acrobatics	stunts like jumping, tumbling, and balancing
hence	from this time; therefore
conformity	agreement in character or action
leery	suspicious
agony	great pain of body or mind

Summary

Pony thinks about fighting as the gang gets ready for the rumble. He concludes that Darry likes fights because of pride, Soda likes the contest, Steve because of hatred, and Two-Bit to conform. Pony thinks the only good reason to fight is for self-defense. He realizes that he isn't proud of being known as a hood. He doesn't want to end up like the members of the other gangs: mean hoods and future convicts. Pony looks the Socs over as they arrive at the vacant lot, observing how neatly they are dressed, thinking to himself that this is why the Greasers are blamed so much: people judge by looks. As Darry and a Soc get the rumble going, Pony thinks about how ashamed Darry is to be there. Only he and Soda know it. Dally arrives to join the fight just as it starts. Soon the Socs are running. All gang members are bruised and/or cut, including Pony. Dally grabs Pony to go see Johnny. On the way to the hospital, Dally tells Pony that if he is tough and cares only for himself, nothing will hurt him. Dally is upset because Johnny is dying and he gets them into Johnny's room using Two-Bit's switchblade. Johnny tells them fighting is useless and advises Pony to stay gold. Johnny dies with those words. Dally loses control and runs from the room.

Student Directives

1. Tell how Pony and Dally handle Johnny's death.
2. Describe what happens to Pony after Johnny's and Dally's deaths.
3. Discuss how Pony will remember Johnny and Dally.
4. Explain the worries Pony feels when he wakes from his delirious state.

Vocabulary

daze	stunned state of mind
stupor	condition in which senses are dull
feverish	restless or state of risen body temperature
bewildered	filled with uncertainty; confused
impact	a strong effect; striking together
triumph	victory
concussion	brain injury due to a blow or fall

Summary

Pony leaves the hospital in a state of shock, convincing himself that Johnny is not dead. He wanders around for hours until a man gives him a ride home. He tells the gang about Johnny and Dally even though his mind is in a haze. Just then, Dally calls. He's headed for the vacant lot. The cops are after him because he's just robbed a store. The gang, Dally, and the police reach the lot at the same time. As Dally pulls out the unloaded gun he'd been carrying, the police shoot and kill him. Although Dally won't be called a hero, Pony will always remember how he risked his life for him and Johnny. He died gallantly. And Johnny would always be his buddy. Pony passes out and spends the next several days sleeping and delirious. When he awakens, Darry and Soda, who have been watching over him constantly, fill him in on everything he can't remember. Pony worries about missing school and the track meets, but he worries most that he may not have asked for Darry.

Idioms

The Outsiders is written just as Pony and his friends speak in everyday conversation. Slang words, phrases and idioms are commonly found in the book as Pony tells the story. Idioms are expressions that are made up of groups of words which must be learned as a whole. The meaning of the words used separately would not translate into the intended idea. For example, when Pony says that Soda never cracks a book at all, he means that Soda doesn't ever read.

Directions: After each idiom, write its meaning.

1. I'd hate to be the Soc who takes a crack at him. (p. 132)

2. ...I'm marked lousy. (p. 132)

3. Soda was keeping up a steady stream of wisecracks. (p. 133)

4. I'd hate to see the day when I had to get my nerve from a can. (p. 137)

5. He looked at me as if I was off my nut. (p. 137)

6. You two blow at the first sign of trouble. (p. 137)

7. He's gonna be asked to start the fireworks around here. (p. 1139-140)

8. They looked like they were all cut from the same piece of cloth. (p. 141)

9. I wasn't exactly itching for someone to break the record. (p. 143)

10. The Soc... was slugging the sense out of me. (p. 144)

11. Tim Shepard was swearing blue and green. (p. 145)

12. I sat tight as Dally roared the car down the street. (p. 146)

13. We all left the house at a dead run. (p. 153)

14. The ground rushed up to meet me very suddenly. (p. 155)

15. He landed all over that Soc. (p. 157)

Student Directives

1. Describe the part of Bob's personality that Pony finally understands.
2. Tell why Randy goes to see Pony.
3. Discuss why Pony insists he is guilty of Bob's murder at this point in the story.

Vocabulary

vague	not clearly expressed
idol	image worshipped as a god; much loved person
environment	surroundings; conditions which may affect development
cocky	very sure of oneself
shrugged	hunch up shoulders to express uncertainty
hot-tempered	easily angered
guardian	a person who legally has the care of another person

Summary

Pony must stay in bed a week. During this time, he comes across a picture of Bob in an old yearbook. After much thinking, Pony concludes that Bob was an angry kid who was both cocky and scared. When Randy visits, he tries to tell Pony that he knows he didn't do anything wrong concerning Bob's death. But Pony, still mixed up emotionally, insists that he himself killed Bob and that Johnny is not dead. He also thinks to himself that Randy is cold-blooded like all other Socs. Darry asks Randy to leave because Pony is getting upset. The exchange between Darry and Pony at this point shows that they are starting to understand each other better.

Student Directives

1. Relate how, after the hearing, Pony's life was still not "back to normal."

2. Describe Pony's reaction when provoked by angry Socs after school.

3. Tell what Soda does to help improve Darry and Pony's relationship.

4. Review Johnny's interpretation of Robert Frost's poem, "Nothing Gold."

5. Discuss the theme Pony chose to write about.

Vocabulary

flinch   to draw back from

desert (v)   to leave without intent to return

acquitted   declared innocent of a crime

roundabout   not direct

reference   writing that directs the reader to other information sources

granted (take for) assumed

Summary

Pony is acquitted and allowed to remain with Darry and Soda. Pony goes back to school but can't get back to normal. His grades, especially in English, are poor. Pony's English teacher tells him that if he can write a good semester theme, then he'll pass with a "C." When some angry Socs come up to Pony in a store lot at lunch one day, he breaks off the end of his soda bottle and threatens them, repeating Dally's words to himself: if you get tough, you don't get hurt. That night Darry and Pony have another fight and Soda runs out. Darry and Pony never realized that they were constantly putting Soda in the middle. He explains how he sees both sides and this brings the brothers closer. Later Pony finds a hopeful note from Johnny in the copy of *Gone With the Wind.* Johnny tells Pony he believes that there is still good in the world and hopes Pony can pass this on to Dally. Pony decides to write his theme paper on the story of boys like his gang: boys who were judged by the amount of hair oil they wore, but maybe watched sunsets and hoped for a better life.

Plot Development

Organization of the plot is crucial to the success of a novel. As the story progresses, the plot moves toward a turning point, or climax. It can be pictured as a hill with the climax as the summit. The action "rises" as the reader gains more information and the conflicts are developed, all leading to the high point (climax). This high point is the event(s) that changes the character's behavior or attitude. It is what the action has been rising toward. The result of this climax, which is called falling action, follows. This is where the changes happen. The falling action ends with the resolution, or final solving of the conflicts. The plot organization is more easily understood when it is set on an organization map.

Directions: Use the Plot Organization map to plot the order of events as they occurred in the story.

- Pony reads Johnny's letter telling him to stay gold

- Pony is jumped

- The church burns and Pony and Johnny save kids

- Pony gets sick

- Pony writes a theme to let others know that the Greasers are people with feelings and hopes, too

- Pony and Johnny meet the girls at the movies

- Soda tells Darry and Pony what their fighting does to him

- Pony and Johnny go into hiding

- Rumble

- Johnny and Dally die

- Pony realizes that Socs are just people who have problems sometimes, too

- The Socs attack Pony and Johnny

- Johnny and Dally are in the hospital

Name _____

Plot Organization Map

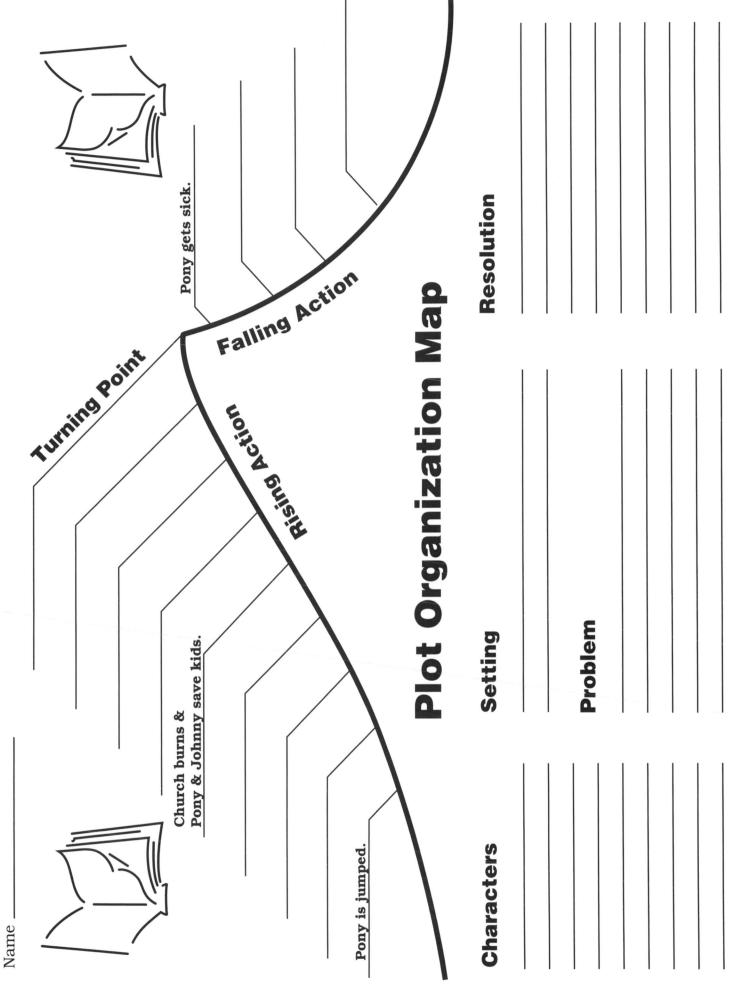

Rising Action

Pony is jumped.

Church burns & Pony & Johnny save kids.

Turning Point

Falling Action

Pony gets sick.

Characters

_____
_____
_____
_____

Setting

_____
_____
_____

Problem

_____
_____
_____
_____
_____

Resolution

_____
_____
_____
_____
_____
_____
_____

Character Development

S.E. Hinton presents a variety of contrasting characters in *The Outsiders*. We learn about the strengths, and weaknesses, of their character through Hinton's narrative, conversations between characters, and through their actions. Pony, Darry, and Soda exemplify the importance of responsibility and honesty in a family. We see, too, that friendships can exist within and between social classes. Even Dally, who seems to care about very little, has some standards when it comes to his friends and horse racing.

Good literature, like *The Outsiders*, provides us with experiences which not only entertain and educate us, but also enrich us spiritually. Hopefully, these experiences develop our own virtues of character. *The Outsiders* gives us many examples of character as models from which we can strive to conduct our own lives.

The Discovering Literature Series focuses on ten virtues of character:

Responsibility	Friendship
Courage	Persistence
Compassion	Hard Work
Loyalty	Self-discipline
Honesty	Faith

Character Development Activity, Page 1

Directions: Choose a character(s) from *The Outsiders* who models the virtue listed below. Briefly explain, using examples from the book, how your character(s) displays each virtue.

Responsibility

_____
character

_____
_____
_____
_____

Courage

_____
character

_____
_____
_____
_____

Compassion

_____
character

_____
_____
_____
_____

Loyalty

_____
character

_____
_____
_____
_____

Character Development Activity, Page 2

Honesty

_____
character

_____

_____

_____

_____

Friendship

_____
character

_____

_____

_____

_____

Persistence

_____
character

_____

_____

_____

_____

Hard Work

_____
character

_____

_____

_____

_____

Self-discipline

_____
character

_____

_____

_____

_____

Issues

1. Pages 77 and 148 and 178. Pony recites Robert Frost's poem, "Nothing Gold Can Stay" to Johnny and they talk about its meaning. Use information from the book to explain what "being gold" means. Why does Johnny tell Pony to "stay gold"? How can you be gold?

   OR

   What would Johnny have said to Dally in a letter about "being gold"? What advice would Johnny have given Dally that would make sense in Dally's life? Use information from the book as you write a letter from Johnny to Dally explaining what "being gold" means.

2. Page 137. Pony tried drinking once and it made him sick. He says he doesn't want to get his nerve from a can, like Two-Bit, who gets drunk before doing anything. There can be many side effects from excessive drinking. List four of the other reasons Pony won't ever drink again. Tell whether you agree with Pony's decision not to drink, using information from the book and knowledge you may already have from your reading or observation.

3. Page 137. Pony tries to understand why each member of the gang fights. He figures out that Soda fights for fun, Steve because of hatred, Darry for his pride and Two-Bit for conformity. As for himself, Pony doesn't think there is any really good reason to fight except self-defense. Do you think any of these reasons are good ones or do you agree with Pony? Explain your answer and use an example from experience or observation.

4. Page 141. Pony believes that the Greasers are always blamed for trouble and Socs never are because the Socs look decent and the Greasers look hoody. Underneath, he knows it could be the other way around, but people usually go by looks. Do you think this is true? Relate an experience you or someone close to you had in which a person judged another by looks or an experience in which a person could have been, but was not, judged by their looks. What was the situation? How did it work out?

TEST

Name _____

Multiple Choice

Directions:

Circle the letter of the

correct answer.

1. Darry doesn't think Pony should be in the rumble because
    A. Johnny isn't there to help him.
    B. it takes place on a school night.
    C. Pony seems to have lost his strength.

2. Pony compares Darry and himself to those Greasers like Tim Shepard and the Brumly boys. What is the difference?
    A. The Shepard and Brumly boys grew up in worse neighborhoods.
    B. Pony and Darry will "get somewhere" in life.
    C. The Shepard and Brumly boys are afraid to fight the Socs.

3. Pony feels different before this rumble because he is
    A. no longer proud of being considered a hood and doesn't want to fight.
    B. worrying about his grades.
    C. angrier than ever at the Socs.

4. Just before he dies, Johnny tells Dally and Pony that fighting is
    A. something he'll miss.
    B. useless.
    C. the only way to settle things.

5. Dally died
    A. only a few days after Johnny.
    B. a hero to Johnny and Pony.
    C. in the rumble.

6. Randy comes to see Pony because he
    A. wants to talk about the hearing
    B. is still angry at Pony.
    C. just found out that Johnny died.

7. Pony doesn't want to admit to himself that Johnny is dead because he

    A. will have to go to the hearing.

    B. will have to remember the fire.

    C. misses Johnny too much.

8. At the hearing, Pony is

    A. fined.

    B. questioned about Bob's murder.

    C. acquitted.

9. After the hearing,

    A. Pony does poorly in school.

    B. Pony's life goes back to normal.

    C. Pony goes to live in another city.

10. Pony finally realizes that

    A. Soda is in the middle of his and Darry's fights.

    B. he should drop out of school and get a job.

    C. the sunsets are different on their side of town.

Vocabulary

Directions:

Fill in the blank with the correct word.

conformity	acquitted	vague
leery	interfere	guardian
prime	bewildered	vast
flinch		

1. _____ declared innocent of a crime

2. _____ suspicious

3. _____ take part in the concerns of others

4. _____ agreement in character or action

5. _____ filled with uncertainty; confused

6. _____ very great in size or amount

Name _____

7. _____ not clearly expressed

8. _____ first in importance, rank, or quality

9. _____ a person who legally has the care of another person

10. _____ to draw back from

Essay Questions

Directions:

Answer in complete

sentences.

1. Explain why the rumble was fought and what it does to change things between the Greasers and the Socs.

   _____

   _____

   _____

2. Dally gives Pony this advice: "Get tough...and nothing can hurt you..." Tell why you agree or disagree, using examples from the book.

   _____

   _____

   _____

3. Give examples from the story to show why Johnny didn't fit the stereotype of a Greaser.

   _____

   _____

   _____

CHAPTER SUMMARY & VOCABULARY | The Outsiders

Chapter Title ______________________ Name ______________________

Chapter Summary:

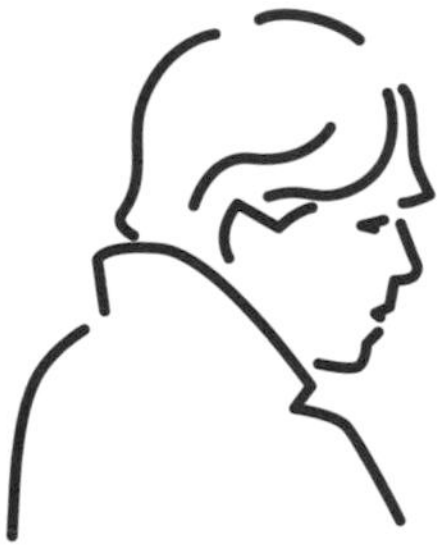

Chapter Vocabulary:

1. ______________________

2. ______________________

3. ______________________

4. ______________________

5. ______________________

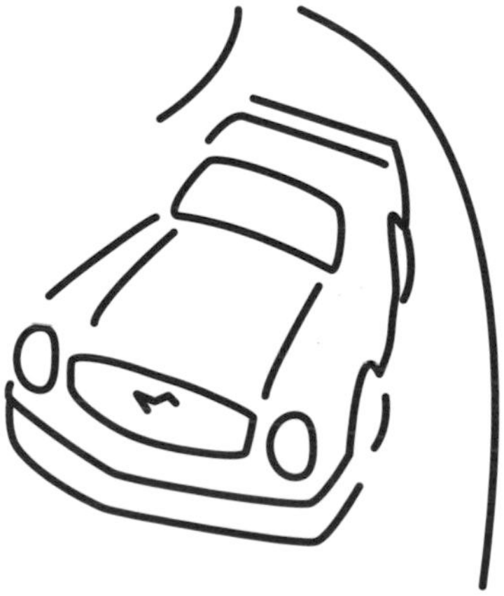

NAME: _____

The Outsiders

The Outsiders

Skill Page: About the Characters, page 9.

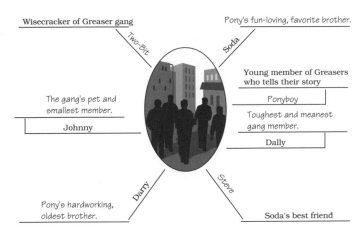

Wisecracker of Greaser gang — Two-Bit

Pony's fun-loving, favorite brother. — Soda

The gang's pet and smallest member. — Johnny

Young member of Greasers who tells their story — Ponyboy

Toughest and meanest gang member. — Dally

Pony's hardworking, oldest brother. — Darry

Soda's best friend — Steve

Skill Page: Compare/Contrast, page 13.

SOCS		GREASERS
Differences	Similarities	Differences

liked Beatles — liked Elvis
girls didn't act tough — girls acted tough
had money — were poor
didn't reveal emotions — were emotional

can get good grades
can watch sunsets
can form friendships
like the same cars
have problems

Accept reasonable answers

Skill Page: Narrative Outline, page 17.

Main Character - Ponyboy

A. Pony is a good student who likes movies and books
B. For a long time, Pony thinks he's the only one who likes sunsets
C. Pony's brothers and gang are important to him
D. Pony wishes there were no social groups

Setting

A. Where: a large town in Oklahoma
B. When: 1960's-70's (inference)

Conflicts

A. Socs vs. Greasers: gang rivalry
B. Pony vs. Darry: Pony didn't think Darry cared about him; they seem to see things differently

C. Greasers vs. Society: Greasers seem to have all the problems and tough breaks

Plot

A. Pony and Johnny will stay at the church until Dally tells Soda and Darry where they are
B. Johnny will go to trial but get off for self-defense
C. The Socs and Greasers won't fight for a long time because Cherry will talk them out of it

Accept reasonable answers.

Skill Page: Cause and Effect, page 18.

1. D 4. J 7. B 10. K
2. I 5. F 8. H 11. C
3. A 6. E 9. G

Test, Chapters 1-4, pages 19–21.

Multiple Choice

1. B   6. A
2. A   7. C
3. A   8. B
4. B   9. C
5. B   10. A

Vocabulary

1. hesitation   6. hastily
2. gallant   7. reputation
3. apprehensive   8. suspicious
4. resignedly   9. defiance
5. rivalry   10. rank

Essay Questions

1. Pony likes movies and books that he can "get into". Pony likes sunsets. Pony gets good grades. Pony likes to draw portraits. Sometimes Pony cries. Pony talks about the horse Mickey Mouse with tenderness. Pony doesn't want to talk rudely to the girls at the movie. Dally's talk embarrasses him. Pony doesn't like to get into fights, and says he couldn't cut anyone. Pony cares about his brothers and his friends. Pony thinks the Greasers deserve a lot of their trouble. He is scared when the Socs jump him.

2. Darry scolds Pony for not using common sense. Darry wants Pony to get good grades and do well in sports. It seems to Pony that Darry is always hollering at him about something, so Pony says, "Me and Darry just didn't dig each other."

3. The Socs were angry because Johnny and Pony picked up their girls; they were drunk and bored, too.

Accept reasonable answers.

Skill Page: Metaphors, page 23.

1. She is saying sweet, nice things.
2. It is raining very hard and noisy like when cats and dogs fight.
3. A fortress is strong and protects.. Therefore, he is my protector.
4. Nature's first green is precious and valuable as is gold.
5. Flowers are the prettiest, most valued part of a plant or tree. Our youth, like a flower, doesn't last long. We should value it and try to remember the good things we enjoy like sunsets instead of letting the bad parts of life overwhelm us.
6. To young people, life is new and they may pay more attention to and enjoy things that older people ignore or are too busy or too overwhelmed with life's difficulties to enjoy.

Skill Page: Sequencing, page 27.

Event 1: Pony is jumped.
Event 2: Dally, Johnny, Pony go to the movies.
Event 3: Two-Bit, Johnny, and Pony start to take Cherry and Marcia home.
Event 4: Pony and Johnny fall asleep in the lot.
Event 5: Darry hits Pony.
Event 6: Pony and Johnny run to the park.
Event 7: The Socs hold Pony's head under water.
Event 8: Dally gives Pony and Johnny money and directions.
Event 9: Pony and Johnny go to Windrixville.
Event 10: Pony and Johnny save some kids.
Event 11: Darry, Soda, and Pony are interviewed for the newspaper.
Event 12: Randy talks to Pony.
Event 13: Two-Bit and Pony visit Johnny in the hospital.
Event 14: Dally asks for Two-Bit's switchblade.
Event 15: Two-Bit and Pony meet Cherry in the vacant lot.

Skill Page: Identifying Characters, page 28.

1. Pony	11. Johnny
2. Soda	12. Steve
3. Pony	13. Darry
4. Johnny	14. Two-Bit
5. Darry	15. Dally
6. Two-Bit	16. Darry
7. Johnny	17. Soda
8. Dally	18. Dally
9. Cherry	19. Pony
10. Pony	20. Cherry

Writer's Forum: Problems of Socs and Greasers, page 29.

Greasers: The Greasers have little money, the reputation of being mean and dirty, and often bad family lives and fewer opportunities than other people.

Socs: The Socs are often spoiled; their parents won't set limits for them. They have too much time because they don't have to work. This allows them the time to cause trouble. Socs are expected to be "cool" and have the pressure to remain popular.

Test, Chapters 5-8, pages 30–32.
Multiple Choice

1. B	6. B
2. B	7. C
3. A	8. C
4. B	9. A
5. C	10. C

Vocabulary

1. sullen	6. indignant
2. conviction	7. fiend
3. divert	8. scowl
4. aghast	9. hue
5. grim	10. elude

Essay Questions

1. Mr. Wood calls Pony and Johnny and Dally professional heroes and says they're sent from heaven. Greasers have the reputation of being mean and unfeeling, but after Mr. Wood sees them risk their lives for others, he can't believe the boys could really be involved with a murder.

2. Cherry becomes a spy for the Greasers because she wants to help them. She likes Pony and he understands her. Because Cherry thinks Pony is nice and there are few nice kids around, she wants to help by letting the Greasers know what the Socs are planning to do at the rumble. She also hopes Pony would help her if he had the chance. Cherry realizes the Greasers and Socs aren't so different: she knows Pony likes sunsets, too, and she's attracted to Dally. Since Cherry hates fights, she probably wants the rumble to be as fair as possible so no one else gets hurt.

Accept reasonable answers.

Skill Page: Idioms, page 35.

1. I'd hate to be the Soc who tries to hit him.
2. I'm seen as being no good.
3. Soda was joking continuously.
4. I don't ever want to drink alcohol to gain the courage to do anything.
5. He looked at me as if I were crazy.
6. You two get out of here.
7. He'll be asked to start the rumble.
8. They all looked alike.
9. I wasn't anxious for someone to fight better than my brother.
10. A Soc was hitting me very hard.
11. Tim Shepard was swearing loudly and continuously.
12. I sat still because the car was moving fast and recklessly.
13. We left the house running as fast as we could.
14. I passed out or fainted.
15. He beat up the Soc without any restraint.

Skill Page: Plot Development, page 38–39.

Name _____

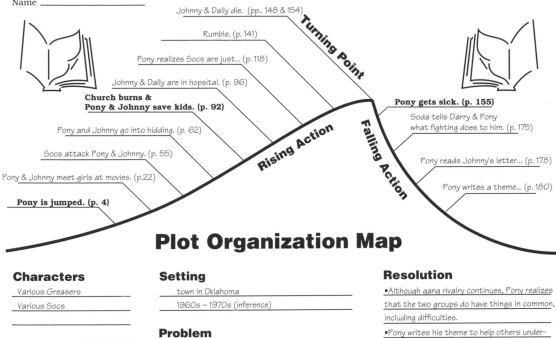

Plot Organization Map

- Johnny & Dally die. (pp.. 148 & 154)
- Rumble. (p. 141)
- Pony realizes Socs are just... (p. 118)
- Johnny & Dally are in hopsital. (p. 96)
- **Church burns & Pony & Johnny save kids. (p. 92)**
- Pony and Johnny go into hidding. (p. 62)
- Socs attack Pony & Johnny. (p. 55)
- Pony & Johnny meet girls at movies. (p.22)
- **Pony is jumped. (p. 4)**

Turning Point

Rising Action

Falling Action

- **Pony gets sick. (p. 155)**
- Soda tells Darry & Pony what fighting does to him. (p. 175)
- Pony reads Johnny's letter... (p. 178)
- Pony writes a theme... (p. 180)

Characters
Various Greasers
Various Socs
_____
_____
_____
_____
_____

Setting
town in Oklahoma
1960s – 1970s (inference)

Problem
• Gang rivalry–Socs vs. Greasers
• Pony & Darry–understanding each other
• Greasers in society–believe they have all the problems

Resolution
• Although gang rivalry continues, Pony realizes that the two groups do have things in common, including difficulties.
• Pony writes his theme to help others understand what he now knows.
• With Soda's help, Pony & Darry realize their fighting is useless & hurtful. They resolve to get along. Pony realizes that Darry loves him.

Skill Page: Character Development, pages 40–42.

Possible answers to support virtues:

Responsibility:
-Soda and Darry both held jobs to help pay bills and stay together as a family.
-All the brothers help around the house.

Courage:
-Pony and Johnny go into the burning church without thinking of themselves.

Compassion:
-Cherry tries to help the Greasers.

Loyalty:
-All the gang members stand by each other when difficulties arise. For example, at the hearing, Soda and Darry are honest about their friendship with Dally even though they fear it may cause Pony trouble.

Honesty:
-Dally rides the ponies in races without fixing the outcome..
-Cherry tells the truth in court.
-Soda tells Darry and Pony how he feels when they fight.

Friendship:
-Johnny was a good friend to Pony, listening and talking to him and defending him.

Persistence:
-Pony keeps trying until he comes up with a good topic for his theme.

Hard Work:
-Darry works very hard to support his family.

Self-discipline:
-Even though everyone around him smoked, Darry refused to because he knew it would hurt his health.
-Pony kept his grades up (before he misses so much school) by faithfully doing his homework.

Test, Chapters 9-12, pages 44–46.

Multiple Choice

1. C
2. B
3. A
4. B
5. B

6. A
7. C
8. C
9. A
10. A

Vocabulary

1. acquitted
2. leery
3. interfere
4. conformity
5. bewildered

6. vast
7. vague
8. prime
9. guardian
10. flinch

Essay Questions

1. The Socs fight the rumble because they want to get back at the Greasers for killing Bob. The Greasers fight because they want to settle the issue of who is better once and for all. What it does to change things between the groups is nothing. The Socs are still the wealthy, more privileged, and more trusted by society. The Greasers still have the reputation of all being hoods. Except for Pony, Cherry, Johnny, and Randy, the two groups still view each other this way, too.

2. Possible example: We know that inside Pony is not tough and he gets hurt by Johnny's death. Dally was tough and he ended up getting hurt, too. So his toughness didn't keep pain from touching him.

3. Johnny didn't fit the stereotype of a greaser because most of the time (except when he pretended in front of the Socs), he had a defeated look in his eye. He was quiet and polite to girls. He didn't pick fights, but his parents beat him. Johnny seemed the most satisfied when he unselfishly ran into the church to save the kids. This contradicts the idea that all Greasers only care for themselves. He liked the sunrise and he told Pony that fighting is useless and to stay gold. Johnny is not proud of killing Bob.

Accept reasonable answers.

ENGLISH SERIES

The **Straight Forward English** series is designed to measure, teach, review, and master specific English skills. All pages are reproducible and include answers to exercises and tests.

Capitalization & Punctuation
GP-032 • 40 pages
I and First Words; Proper Nouns; Ending Marks and Sentences; Commas; Apostrophes; Quotation Marks.

Nouns & Pronouns
GP-033 • 40 pages
Singular and Plural Nouns; Common and Proper Nouns; Concrete and Abstract Nouns; Collective Nouns; Possessive Pronouns; Pronouns and Contractions; Subject and Object Pronouns.

Verbs
GP-034 • 40 pages
Action Verbs; Linking Verbs; Verb Tense; Subject-Verb Agreement; Spelling Rules for Tense; Helping Verbs; Irregular Verbs; Past Participles.

Sentences
GP-041 • 40 pages
Sentences; Subject and Predicate; Sentence Structures.

Adjectives & Adverbs
GP-035 • 40 pages
Proper Adjectives; Articles; Demonstrative Adjectives; Comparative Adjectives; Special Adjectives: Good and Bad; -ly Adverbs; Comparative Adverbs; Good-Well and Bad-Badly.

Prepositions, Conjunctions and Interjections
GP-043 • 40 pages
Recognizing Prepositions; Object of the Preposition; Prepositional Phrases; Prepositional Phrases as Adjectives and Adverbs; Faulty Reference; Coordinating, Correlative and Subordinate Conjunctions.

ADVANCED ENGLISH SERIES

Get It Right!
GP-148 • 144 pages
Organized into four sections, **Get It Right!** is designed to teach writing skills commonly addressed in the standardized testing in the early grades: Spelling, Mechanics, Usage, and Proofreading. Overall the book includes 100 lessons, plus reviews and skill checks.

All-In-One English
GP-107 • 112 pages
The **All-In-One** is a master book to the Straight Forward English Series.
Under one cover it has included the important English skills of capitalization, punctuation, and all eight parts of speech. Each selection of the All-In-One explains and models a skill and then provides focused practice, periodic review, and testing to help measure acquired skills. Progress through all skills is thorough and complete.

Grammar Rules!
GP-102 • 250 pages
Grammar Rules! is a straightforward approach to basic English grammar and English writing skills. Forty units each composed of four lessons for a total of 160 lessons, plus review, skill checks, and answers. Units build skills with Parts of Speech, Mechanics, Diagramming, and Proofreading. Solid grammar and writing skills are explained, modeled, practiced, reviewed, and tested.

Clauses & Phrases
GP-055 • 80 pages
Adverb, Adjective and Noun Clauses; Gerund, Participial and Infinitive Verbals; Gerund, Participial, Infinitive, Prepositional and Appositive Phrases.

Mechanics
GP-056 • 80 pages
Abbreviations; Apostrophes; Capitalization; Italics; Quotation Marks; Numbers; Commas; Semicolons; Colons; Hyphens; Parentheses; Dashes; Brackets; Ellipses; Slashes.

Grammar & Diagramming Sentences
GP-075 • 110 pages
The Basics; Diagramming Rules and Patterns; Nouns and Pronouns; Verbs; Modifiers; Prepositions, Conjunctions, and Special Items; Clauses and Compound-Complex Sentences.

Troublesome Grammar
GP-019 • 120 pages •
Agreement; Regular and Irregular Verbs; Modifiers; Prepositions and Case, Possessives and Contractions; Plurals; Active and Passive Voice; Comparative Forms; Word Usage; and more.

Math Series

The Straight Forward Math Series

is systematic, first diagnosing skill levels, then *practice*, periodic *review*, and *testing*.

Blackline

GP-006 Addition
GP-012 Subtraction
GP-007 Multiplication
GP-013 Division
GP-039 Fractions
GP-083 Word Problems, Book 1
GP-042 Word Problems, Book 2

The Advanced Straight Forward Math Series

is a higher level system to diagnose, practice, review, and test skills.

Blackline

GP-015 Advanced Addition
GP-016 Advanced Subtraction
GP-017 Advanced Multiplication
GP-018 Advanced Division
GP-020 Advanced Decimals
GP-021 Advanced Fractions
GP-044 Mastery Tests
GP-025 Percent
GP-028 Pre-Algebra, Book 1
GP-029 Pre-Algebra, Book 2
GP-030 Pre-Geometry, Book 1
GP-031 Pre-Geometry, Book 2
GP-163 Pre-Algebra Companion

Upper Level Math Series

GP-104 Algebra, Book 1
GP-105 Algebra, Book 2
GP-045 Trigonometry
GP-054 Geometry
GP-053 Pre-Calculus
GP-064 Calculus AB, Vol. 1
GP-067 Calculus AB, Vol. 2

Math Pyramid Puzzles

Math Pyramid Puzzles
ISBN 978-1-9308-2062-3
GP-162
5 two-sided puzzles

Assemble 5 two-sided puzzles each with different mathematical challenges. Solve the mathematical pyramid on the front side, turn the clear tray over to reveal of problem of logic: percents, decimals, fractions, exponents and factors.

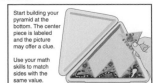

Start building your pyramid at the bottom. The center piece is labeled and the picture may offer a clue.

Use your math skills to match sides with the same value.

You may find more than one match, but **all sides that touch** must match. When you are satisfied with your solution, close the tray.

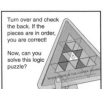

Turn over and check the back. If the pieces are in order, you are correct!

Now, can you solve this logic puzzle?